The MAILBOX®

The Education Center®

Read-Along Roundup

Preschool

A bonanza of learning activities based on 50 favorite books!

⭐ **Literacy activities**

⭐ **Math activities**

⭐ **Science activities**

⭐ **Social studies activities**

⭐ **Art activities**

⭐ **Discussion questions**

⭐ **Patterns**

Managing Editors: Kimberly Brugger-Murphy and Tina Petersen

Editorial Team: Becky S. Andrews, Diane Badden, Kimberley Bruck, Karen A. Brudnak, Pam Crane, Elizabeth A. Cook, Roxanne LaBell Dearman, Brenda Fay, Pierce Foster, Ada Goren, Tazmen Hansen, Marsha Heim, Lori Z. Henry, Debra Liverman, Kitty Lowrance, Mark Rainey, Hope Rodgers, Donna K. Teal, Rachael Traylor, Sharon M. Tresino

www.themailbox.com

©2011 The Mailbox® Books
All rights reserved.
ISBN10 #1-56234-985-6 • ISBN13 #978-1-56234-985-1

Printed in the United States
10 9 8 7 6 5 4 3 2 1

HPS227023

Table of Contents

50 featured read-alouds!

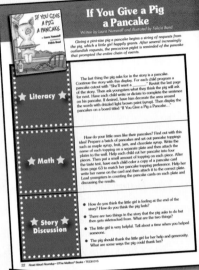

100 activities!

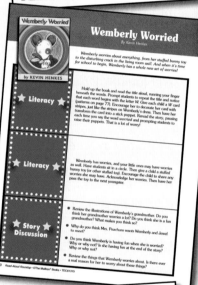

181 discussion questions!

25 pattern and reproducible pages!

All of this in an easy-to-read format!

Bark, George
By Jules Feiffer

George meows, quacks, oinks, and moos, but he does not bark as a dog should. However, the vet knows exactly how to remove George's problem.

★ Literacy ★

This entertaining story lends itself to a giggle-inducing reenactment. Assign roles to your youngsters and reread the story aloud. When George's mother takes him to see the vet, have the appropriate students line up behind George. After the vet asks George to bark, have the student directly behind George make her character's sound. Then have the vet take her hand and lead her past George to simulate the removal!

★ Science ★

What other animals could be inside George? Little ones find out during this enjoyable activity. To prepare a George prop, draw a simple dog face on a small paper bag and then glue on two paper ears. Cut out a copy of the animal cards on page 55 and place them in the bag. Invite a volunteer to pretend to be the vet. Have him remove a card, name the animal, and lead the group in making that animal's sound. Continue until all the cards have been used.

★ Story Discussion ★

● What do you think it means when George says, "Hello"? What do you think George's mom will do now?

● What would you do if your pet started making a different animal's sound?

● How do you think the animals got inside George?

Barnyard Banter

By Denise Fleming

Almost all the boisterous barnyard animals are making the expected noises in their expected places. But where is Goose? She's chasing a butterfly through the pages of this colorful story!

★ Literacy ★

Youngsters will create their own barnyard banter with this lively activity. Help them determine the meaning of the word *banter*, looking back in the story as needed. Then revisit the page that shows all the animal sounds at once. Invite each child to choose an animal from the story. When the signal is given, have youngsters simultaneously make their animals' sounds. If desired, encourage each child to choose a different animal and repeat the activity.

★ Art ★

Denise Fleming uses paper pulp to create unique illustrations, and your youngsters can too! Have youngsters cut newspaper into small pieces. When you have a bowl of newspaper pieces, add water and let them soak overnight. The next day, have each child reach in the bowl and squish and squeeze the paper until it is the consistency of oatmeal. Drain any excess water; then add glue and salt to the mixture. Invite students to spread and mold the mixture on a piece of cardboard. When it is dry, have them paint the paper pulp. What fun!

★ Story Discussion ★

- What is Goose chasing throughout the book? What do you think Goose would do if she caught the butterfly?

- All the characters in the story make a sound except for the butterfly. What sound do you think a butterfly would make if it could make noise?

- Each animal makes its own distinctive sound. Do you think different animals can understand each other?

Big Fat Hen

Illustrated by Keith Baker

The vibrant illustrations and familiar text of this delightful rhyme will have little ones clucking to hear it again and again.

★ Literacy ★

Enlist youngsters' help in giving this classic rhyme a new twist. Reread the book, guiding youngsters to recognize the rhyming words in each couplet. Then, on a sheet of chart paper, write the first couplet of the rhyme, omitting the word *shoe*. Invite a volunteer to name a different word that rhymes with *two*. Continue in this manner with each remaining couplet. After all the couplets are complete, lead the students in reading the new rhyme. You're sure to hear lots of giggles!

★ Math ★

Where will the hens keep all those little chicks? Why, in chicken coops, of course. Gather a supply of yellow pom-poms (chicks). Place the chicks near two yarn circles (coops). Invite two youngsters to pretend to be hens. Have each hen place a few chicks in separate coops. Then lead the group in counting the chicks in each coop and in comparing the amounts, using the words *more*, *less*, and *equal*. Choose two more youngsters and play another round.

★ Story Discussion ★

- This version of the rhyme has an extra ending added by the illustrator. Do you like the ending? What ending would you add to the rhyme?

- Imagine you are a chick inside an egg. What do you think it would be like inside the egg? How would you feel after hatching?

- Big Fat Hen and her friends have lots of little chicks to entertain. What kinds of games or activities do you think they might do together?

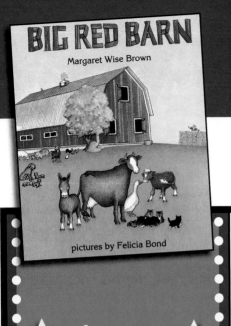

Big Red Barn

Written by Margaret Wise Brown and illustrated by Felicia Bond

Visit the big red barn in the great green field to meet farm animals of every shape and size. From the tiny squeaking mice to the large lowing cow, the animals go about their day doing things that animals do.

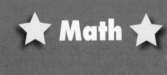

The animals live in the big red barn just as your little ones live in houses. Have students compare the two with this activity! On the board draw an outline of a house and an outline of a barn. Ask little ones to name some things they do in and around their homes. Write their responses in the house. Then ask the group to name things that animals do in and around the barn. Write these responses in the barn. Help youngsters compare the two lists and notice any responses that are similar.

★ Math ★

This soothing tale has animals of every size! During a rereading of the story, direct youngsters to listen for the words *big* and *little*. Each time a child hears the word *big*, have him spread his arms out wide. Each time he hears the word *little*, have him hold his hands up so there is only a small space between them.

- In this story, the children are away and only the animals are there that day. Where do you think the children might be?

- A farmer is not mentioned in the story. Who do you think takes care of the animals? Do you think the animals take care of themselves?

- This story is often read to children as a bedtime story. Why do you think that is so?

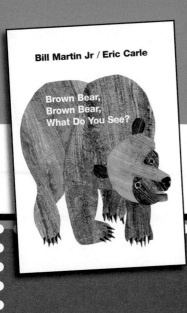

Bill Martin Jr / Eric Carle

Brown Bear, Brown Bear, What Do You See?

Brown Bear, Brown Bear, What Do You See?

Written by Bill Martin Jr. and illustrated by Eric Carle

A series of colorful and unusual sightings begins as Brown Bear spies a red bird in this catchy chant.

★ Literacy ★

Encourage little ones to test their memories and recall story details! After reading the story aloud, invite volunteers to name an animal from the story and its color. Write students' responses on a board. During a rereading of the story, place a check next to each listed animal as it appears in the book.

★ Math ★

This classic book is perfect to use for a color-recognition activity. Give each child a color card that matches one of the colors in the book. Read the story aloud and have each child stand and hold up his card when the corresponding animal is mentioned.

★ Story Discussion ★

- The horse and the cat are not portrayed in their natural colors. Why do you think the author chose to make the horse blue and the cat purple?

- Where could the children be that they would see all these animals in one place?

- There is a variety of animals in the story. Do you think they are some of the author's favorite animals? If you were the author, what animals would you use?

Bunny Party

By Rosemary Wells

Ruby has carefully selected her stuffed toy guests for Grandma's birthday party, but thanks to her brother, Max, a few uninvited guests will also be joining the fun.

 **Literacy**

This amusing story is the perfect choice for a reenactment. Place in the dramatic-play area a small table with chairs, stuffed animals, paper plates, paper cups, plastic cutlery, and a copy of the book. Set out props to help Max disguise the uninvited guests. Then encourage youngsters to visit the center and act out the story.

 **Math**

Ruby wants all the guests to have candy in their favor baskets. Invite youngsters to help Ruby prepare the favors for Grandma's party. Gather youngsters around several small baskets on the floor. Provide a variety of colorful manipulatives (candies). Say, "Can't-Sit-Up Slug wants ten candies in its basket." Then have a child place ten candies in a basket. Continue in the same way, using different numbers and character names.

 **Story Discussion**

● Ruby does not invite any of Max's toys to the party. Do you think that is fair of Ruby? Do you think it hurts Max's feelings?

● Max seats three uninvited guests at the table. Do you think Ruby is upset with Max when she realizes what he did? Why or why not?

● Imagine you were planning a party. Who would you invite? What foods would you serve? What games would you play?

● Have you ever hosted a party or been to a party? What happened?

Caps for Sale

By Esphyr Slobodkina

A cap peddler walks with a stack of caps on his head. In need of rest, he naps beneath a tree full of mischievous monkeys, never suspecting that he'll awaken to a surprising turn of events.

★ **Literacy** ★

Youngsters pretend to be mischievous little monkeys during a reenactment of this entertaining tale. Have each child color a cap cutout (pattern on page 56). Then staple the cap to a headband sized to fit her head. To reenact the story, play the role of the peddler and have the little ones play the parts of the monkeys!

★ **Math** ★

The peddler has just the right number of caps so each monkey in the tree has a cap to wear. Enlist youngsters' help in making sure each monkey has a cap to wear in this one-to-one correspondence activity. Cut apart several copies of the monkey and cap cards on page 56. Draw a simple tree on a sheet of bulletin board paper and place the tree at a center. A child places the monkeys in the tree. Then she places a cap above each monkey!

★ **Story Discussion** ★

● Do you think it was a good idea for the peddler to carry his caps on his head, or should he carry them in a sack? How would you carry them?

● The peddler was having trouble selling his caps. What could he do to sell them?

● What things did the peddler do that showed he was angry with the monkeys? What would be a better way of dealing with the problem?

● Imagine you are a peddler. What items would you want to sell? How would you carry your things from place to place?

Story by Ruth Krauss
Pictures by Crockett Johnson

Even though his family is doubtful, the little boy believes that his carrot seed will grow. His patience and hard work pay off when the seed not only sprouts but also grows into a huge carrot.

Literacy

Lead youngsters in the song below to review how the boy helps the seed grow. Sing the first verse. Then repeat it two more times, replacing the underlined words with *pulls out the weeds* and *sprinkles water*. Then sing the final verse.

(sung to the tune of "The Farmer in the Dell")

The boy [plants a seed].
The boy [plants a seed].
They say, "It won't come up."
The boy [plants a seed].

The carrot grows so big.
The carrot grows so big.
Just like he knew it would,
The carrot grows so big.

Science

The boy's large carrot comes from a small seed. Many other things begin as small seeds too. Cut apart a copy of the cards on page 57 and place them in a small bag near a T chart labeled "begins as a seed" and "does not begin as a seed." Invite a child to take a card and name the picture. Then guide the group to determine in which column the card belongs. Continue with the remaining cards.

Story Discussion

● The boy's family continues to tell him that his carrot is not going to come up. How do you think this makes the boy feel? How do you think he feels when he has a large carrot to show for his hard work?

● What are weeds? Why does the little boy pull up the weeds that are growing around his seed?

● The boy's carrot is huge. What do you think he will do with his carrot? What would you do with the carrot?

● The boy has to be patient and wait for his carrot to grow. Discuss a time that you had to be patient.

Cindy Ward
Tomie dePaola

Cookie's Week
Written by Cindy Ward and illustrated by Tomie dePaola

Garbage cans, flowerpots, and kitchen drawers—these are just some of the many things that a cat named Cookie gets into in one week. As the mischievous feline goes from one thing to another, she leaves a messy trail behind.

This entertaining story portrays several examples of cause and effect. Cut apart a copy of the picture cards on page 58 and place them in a small bag. After reading the story aloud, invite a child to take a card and display it for the group. Then ask a volunteer to describe the mischief that caused the mess pictured on the card. Revisit the book to check the answer. Continue with the remaining cards.

What does Cookie do on Sunday? Why, she comes to your classroom, of course! Encourage youngsters to continue her escapades with a class book. For each child, program one side of a sheet of paper with "On _____, Cookie _____." On the other side of the paper, write "There was _____ everywhere!" Invite youngsters to brainstorm mischievous acts that Cookie could do in the classroom. Invite each child to dictate to complete each sentence on his paper. Then direct him to illustrate the sentences. Bind the pages together between two covers. Then read the book aloud to your little ones!

- Tell about a time your pets or someone else's pets got into mischief.

- Who do you think cleans up Cookie's little messes? Do you think that person is happy with Cookie?

- Name jobs pet owners have to do to take care of their pets. Which jobs would you like? Which jobs would you dislike?

- Look at what Cookie is doing on the last two pages of the book. Do you think Cookie is going to do something mischievous? What do you think it will be?

words and pictures by mo willems

Don't Let the Pigeon Drive the Bus!

By Mo Willems

The bus driver in this story leaves his bus under the watchful eyes of the reader with one simple request—don't let the pigeon drive the bus! But the pigeon is determined to get his way.

★ Literacy ★

During the story, youngsters have the important job of keeping an eye on the bus. This requires them to tell the pigeon "No!" when he continually asks if he can drive the bus. These speech bubble props are just what they need to help them out! Give each child a speech bubble cutout. Help him write "No!" on it; then tape a craft stick to its back. During a rereading of the story, direct students to hold up their speech bubbles as they answer the pigeon's appeals.

★ Art ★

Since the pigeon does not get to drive the bus, what will he do next? Youngsters decide what the pigeon's next escapade will be during this activity. Give each child a sheet of white paper and have her make a light-blue handprint on it with her fingers together and thumb extended. (The fingers and palm are the pigeon's body, and the thumb is the neck and head.) Invite her to add details to the pigeon, such as an eye, a beak, a wing, and legs. Then draw a large thought bubble near the pigeon's head and have her draw and describe the pigeon's next escapade.

★ Story Discussion ★

- Have you ever wanted to do something so much that you asked to do it over and over again? What happened?

- Revisit the pages that show the pigeon having a tantrum. Do you think the pigeon is making a good choice? Discuss some better choices he could make.

- The pigeon's emotions change throughout the story. What different emotions does he demonstrate? Do you think you would feel the same as the pigeon if you were in the same situation?

- A large truck appears at the end of the story. What do you think the pigeon will do next?

Five Little Monkeys Jumping on the Bed

By Eileen Christelow

Five little monkeys romp enthusiastically on a bed in this book fashioned after the classic rhyme.

★ Literacy ★

Those little monkeys are at it again! They are jumping into some new antics with unfortunate results. Read the rhyme below and have youngsters fill in the rhyming body part that the monkey bumps as he jumps. Continue with each suggestion given.

Five little monkeys jumping [in some jelly].
One fell down and bumped his [belly].

Continue with the following: *in a tree, knee; in a creek, cheek; on a track, back; on a boulder, shoulder; on a pier, ear*

★ Math ★

Monkeys aren't the only ones that can jump on a bed. Attach masking tape to the floor to make a large rectangle (bed). Invite the youngsters to stand on the bed, leaving plenty of space between each other. Display a number card and ask a volunteer to name the number. Then direct youngsters to count as they jump a matching number of times. When they reach the correct number, encourage them to gently fall down just like the monkeys in the story! Display a different number card to play another round.

★ Story Discussion ★

● Think about your bedtime routine. What are some things you do to get ready for bed?

● What other things could the monkeys do if they have trouble sleeping again?

● The monkeys bump their heads because they do not follow the doctor's orders. What do you think the monkeys learn?

● What are some rules that must be followed at home or at school? Is it hard to obey these rules?

The Flea's Sneeze

Written by Lynn Downey and illustrated by Karla Firehammer

As the other farm animals snooze peacefully, a tiny flea lets out an enormous sneeze. The flustered animals jolt awake, and the mouse gives the flea a tissue. Then they go back to sleep, except for one hog!

★ Literacy ★

Little ones pretend to be the sleeping animals during this amusing reenactment. Ask one student to be the flea. Then invite each remaining child to pretend he is one of the other animals. Have the animals lie down and pretend to sleep as they listen to the story. At the appropriate point in the story, direct the flea to sneeze loudly. Then have the other animals quickly wake up and begin making their sounds. Have the mouse give a tissue to the flea. Then encourage the group to pretend to sleep again as they listen to the rest of the story.

★ Literacy ★

The tiny flea is suffering from a big cold. Little ones send him flea-size get-well wishes with this activity. Display a few get-well cards. Guide youngsters to notice the types of pictures and sentiments on and in the cards. Then give each child a small piece of paper and help her fold it in half. Instruct her to draw and write or dictate to make a get-well card for the flea.

★ Story ★ Discussion

- Review the final page of the story. What do you think could happen next?

- Have you ever had a cold? What were some of the symptoms? How did you feel?

- Have you ever been startled during the night? Tell what happened.

- The flea needs some advice about how to get over his cold. What are some things he could do to feel better?

- Colds are caused by germs. What are some ways to keep from spreading germs?

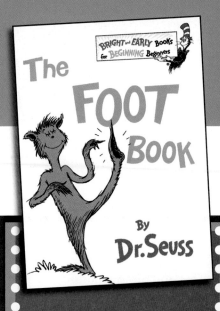

The Foot Book

By Dr. Seuss

Oh my! How many, many feet you meet in this simple Seuss story, which is quite a treat!

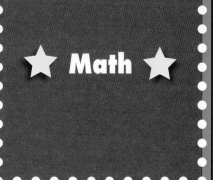 **★ Literacy ★**

Not only are there many feet in this entertaining story, but there also are oodles of feet in your classroom! On a sheet of construction paper, trace a child's feet. Then invite him to decorate the tracing as desired. Have him dictate a label for his feet, such as the following: little feet, green feet, or flowery feet. Write the label on the paper. Display the class's finished papers on a board titled "Meet Our Feet," or bind them together to make a class book with the same title.

★ Math ★

Youngsters learn another meaning of the word *foot* with this measurement activity. In advance, gather a ruler and several common objects. Tell students that a foot isn't just something you put your shoe on; it's also a length used in measurements. Then show the group a ruler and explain that the ruler is equal to a foot. Display one object at a time and ask youngsters if they think it is longer or shorter than a foot. Then hold the ruler next to the object so students can check their answers. Continue with the remaining objects.

 **★ Story Discussion ★**

- Name something that you would wear on your feet. What is your favorite thing to wear on your feet? What is your least favorite thing to wear on your feet?

- Name other animals that have two feet like humans. Name animals that have more than two feet.

- Do you like to go barefoot? When is it okay to go barefoot?

Go Away, Big Green Monster!

By Ed Emberley

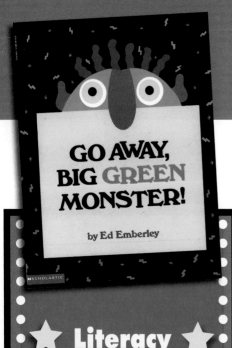

Yikes! Yellow eyes, purple hair, and sharp white teeth sure sound scary. But not to worry! This big green monster doesn't hang around too long. In fact, the big green guy leaves as quickly as he came.

★ Literacy ★

Make a class monster that can appear and disappear as easily as the one in the book. Color and cut out a copy of the patterns on page 59. Then prepare the cutouts for flannelboard use. Display a large green circle on the flannelboard and place the cutouts nearby. Invite a volunteer to add the eyes to the monster. Then lead the group in saying, "Our monster has [two big yellow eyes]."Continue for each facial feature. Once the monster is complete, enlist youngsters' help in removing the features, chanting, "Go away, [facial feature]!" each time.

★ Art ★

The big green monster will not be the only monster in your classroom at the end of this activity. Give each child a colorful construction paper circle (monster head) and access to construction paper scraps. Direct him to use the scraps to add facial details to the monster. Display the monsters and then describe one of them. Ask a volunteer to point to the monster that fits the description. Continue with several different monsters.

★ Story Discussion ★

● Where do you think the monster goes when it leaves the story?

● Are monsters real or make-believe? Why do you think so?

● Study the illustrations in the book. How does the author make the monster appear and disappear?

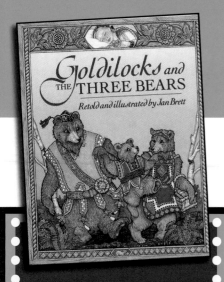

Goldilocks and the Three Bears

Retold and illustrated by Jan Brett

Three bears, three bowls, three beds, three chairs, and one wandering little girl with flaxen braids teach the importance of being a considerate and invited guest.

Literacy

Encourage little ones to study the story's illustrations for specific details. Make a copy of the picture mat on page 60 and attach the page to a table. Provide small bear manipulatives and a copy of the book. Encourage a pair of students to look through the book for the pictured items. When they find one, they place a bear manipulative on the appropriate picture on the mat. Encourage them to continue until they find all the items on the mat.

Math

During their morning walk, each bear gathers a few items. Enlist youngsters' help to place the bears' items in the correct bags. Gather a variety of small, medium, and large household items. Draw a simple small, medium, and large bear head on separate grocery bags. Invite a volunteer to choose an item and decide its size. Then she places it in the appropriate bag. Continue with other volunteers.

Story Discussion

- Porridge is a soft food with a texture similar to oatmeal. Do you think you would like to eat porridge for breakfast? What is your favorite breakfast food?

- Why do you think Goldilocks likes the little bear's things best?

- How do the bears know someone has been using their things? How do you think the bears feel when they find their things have been disturbed?

- Goldilocks is not a polite guest. What could she do to make up for her lack of manners?

Growing Vegetable Soup

By Lois Ehlert

A child and father plant and grow a vegetable garden that provides the ingredients for a pot full of delicious vegetable soup. Each step from what happens in the garden to eating the veggies in the soup is described. Yum!

Written and illustrated by
Lois Ehlert

★ **Literacy** ★

What types of vegetables do little ones think will make a yummy vegetable soup? Show youngsters the cover of the book and read the title aloud. Then invite volunteers to predict which vegetables the father and child will put in the soup. Write youngsters' responses on the board. Then read the book aloud. Revisit the list and check students' predictions, referring to the book as needed.

★ **Art** ★

Encourage youngsters to make vegetable soup the way they like it. Give each child a sheet of red tissue paper, a disposable bowl, and access to a supply of colorful paper scraps. Direct her to cut or tear vegetable shapes from the paper scraps and glue them to the tissue paper. Then have her scrunch the paper and glue it to the inside of the bowl. If desired, have her glue a plastic spoon to the soup. Encourage the child to show her soup to the class and name the ingredients.

★ **Story** ★
Discussion

- What other things could the father and child make with the vegetables? What would you make with the vegetables?

- How do the father and child help the vegetables grow?

- What types of tools do the father and child use when they work in the garden?

- The father and child wash the vegetables before cutting them up. Why is it important to wash vegetables before you eat them?

- Have you ever grown anything? Talk about your experience.

The Hat

By Jan Brett

When a curious hedgehog gets a woolen stocking stuck on his spines, he becomes the laughingstock of all the other animals on the farm. That is until he convinces the animals that they all need similar headwear.

★ Literacy ★

Reinforce the story's plot with a search for winter wear! Put socks, scarves, hats, and mittens on several stuffed toys and place them around the room. Assign a child to play the part of Lisa. Ask a few other youngsters to help Lisa by searching for her winter wear. Direct them to remove the clothing and return it to Lisa. If desired, place the animals and winter wear in a center for independent exploration.

★ Literacy ★

After Lisa retrieves her winter woolens, what will the animals wear as hats? Little ones answer this question with this class book. Cut out several copies of the animal patterns on pages 61 and 62. For each child, program a sheet of paper with the following sentence: "The _____ is wearing _____ as a hat." Each child colors an animal cutout and glues it to a sheet of paper. Then he cuts a desired picture from a magazine and glues it above his animal to make a unique hat! He writes or dictates to complete his sentence. Bind the pages between two covers and read the resulting class book aloud.

★ Story Discussion ★

- Look at the pictures of the house and landscape. Do you think this book takes place where you live? Why or why not?

- How do you think Hedgie feels when the other animals continue to laugh at him? How do you think Hedgie feels near the end of the story?

- Animals normally do not wear clothes. How do they stay warm during the winter?

- Could this story really happen? Which parts could happen? Which parts would not happen?

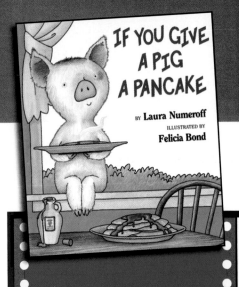

If You Give a Pig a Pancake

Written by Laura Numeroff and illustrated by Felicia Bond

Giving a pint-size pig a pancake begins a string of requests from the pig, which a little girl happily grants. After several increasingly outlandish requests, the precocious piglet is reminded of the pancake that prompted the entire chain of events.

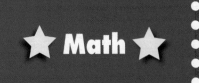

The last thing the pig asks for in the story is a pancake. Continue the story with this display. For each child program a pancake cutout with "She'll want a _____." Revisit the last page of the story. Then ask youngsters what they think the pig will ask for next. Have each child write or dictate to complete the sentence on his pancake. If desired, have him decorate the area around the words with drizzled light brown paint (syrup). Then display the pancakes on a board titled "If You Give a Pig a Pancake…"

Math

How do your little ones like their pancakes? Find out with this idea! Prepare a batch of pancakes and set out pancake toppings such as maple syrup, fruit, jam, and chocolate syrup. Write the name of each topping on a separate plate and then attach the plates to the wall. Help each child cut her pancake into four pieces. Then put a small amount of topping on each piece. After the taste test, have each child color a copy of a pancake card from page 63 to match her pancake topping preference. Help her write her name on the card and then attach it to the correct plate. Lead youngsters in counting the pancake cards on each plate and discussing the results.

Story Discussion

● How do you think the little girl is feeling at the end of the story? How do you think the pig feels?

● There are two things in the story that the pig asks to do but then gets sidetracked from. What are the two things?

● The little girl is very helpful. Tell about a time when you helped someone.

● The pig should thank the little girl for her help and generosity. What are some ways the pig could thank her?

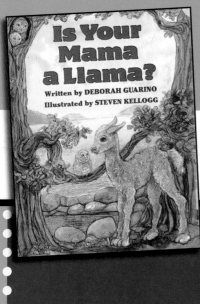

Is Your Mama a Llama?

Written by Deborah Guarino and illustrated by Steven Kellogg

When a baby llama asks other animals about their mothers, he soon learns that only llamas have llama mothers.

Literacy

The animals in the story tell Lloyd the things about their mothers that make them unique. Encourage little ones to practice speaking skills as they tell about their mothers' unique qualities. In advance, have each child bring a photo of her mother from home or draw a picture of her mother. After reading the story aloud, invite each child to share the photo of her mother with the group and tell what makes her mother unique and special.

Science

During the story Lloyd learns many things about his animal friends and their mothers. Cut apart a copy of the cards on page 64 and place them in a small bag. Invite a child to take two cards from the bag and name the animals. Display the cards; then revisit the pages in the story that involve the two animals. Guide youngsters to discuss how the animals are alike and different. Continue with other pairs of cards.

Story Discussion

● Several different animals are mentioned in the story. Which animal in the story would you like to be? Explain your choice.

● Revisit the illustrations. Do you see animals that are not mentioned in the story? Name the animals.

● Many mother animals take care of their babies. How does your mother take care of you?

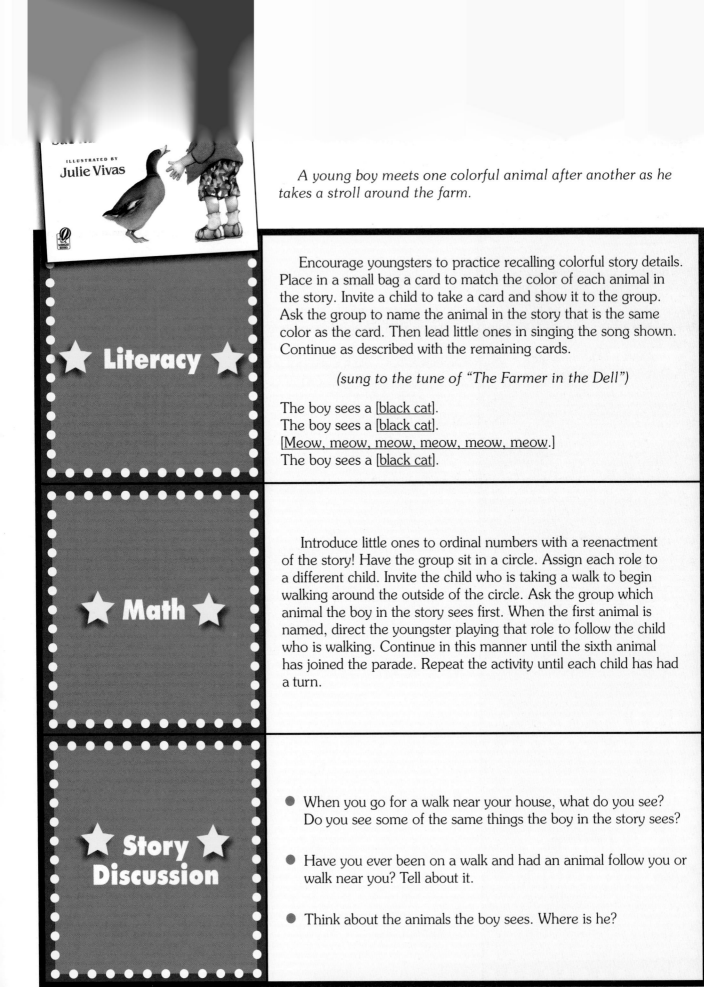

ILLUSTRATED BY
Julie Vivas

A young boy meets one colorful animal after another as he takes a stroll around the farm.

★ Literacy ★

Encourage youngsters to practice recalling colorful story details. Place in a small bag a card to match the color of each animal in the story. Invite a child to take a card and show it to the group. Ask the group to name the animal in the story that is the same color as the card. Then lead little ones in singing the song shown. Continue as described with the remaining cards.

(sung to the tune of "The Farmer in the Dell")

The boy sees a [black cat].
The boy sees a [black cat].
[Meow, meow, meow, meow, meow, meow.]
The boy sees a [black cat].

★ Math ★

Introduce little ones to ordinal numbers with a reenactment of the story! Have the group sit in a circle. Assign each role to a different child. Invite the child who is taking a walk to begin walking around the outside of the circle. Ask the group which animal the boy in the story sees first. When the first animal is named, direct the youngster playing that role to follow the child who is walking. Continue in this manner until the sixth animal has joined the parade. Repeat the activity until each child has had a turn.

★ Story Discussion ★

● When you go for a walk near your house, what do you see? Do you see some of the same things the boy in the story sees?

● Have you ever been on a walk and had an animal follow you or walk near you? Tell about it.

● Think about the animals the boy sees. Where is he?

The Jacket I Wear in the Snow

Written by Shirley Neitzel and illustrated by Nancy Winslow Parker

From her green jacket to her wrinkled socks, this young child is bundled up against the harsh winter weather. It's too bad all those itchy, bunchy layers are so uncomfortable!

Literacy

Before reading the story, encourage little ones to name different kinds of winter apparel. Record their responses on a large snowball cutout. During a read-aloud of the story, put a check mark next to each item on the list that the little girl wears. After the read-aloud, compare the winter wear worn in the story to the list.

Social Studies

With this fun idea, little ones are sure to understand the young girl's plight of bundling up in uncomfortable winter wear! Provide a selection of winter clothing. Also provide wads of cotton batting and large white pom-poms (snow) along with plastic pails and shovels. Youngsters dress themselves for snow play, asking a classmate for help if needed. Once students are dressed, they play together in the faux snow. When they are finished playing, they remove their winter wear.

Story Discussion

- What might the girl be thinking and feeling as she gets dressed to play in the snow? What might she think and feel as she tries to play in the snow wearing the layers of winter clothing?

- What articles of clothing does the little girl put on? What is the best sequence for putting the items on? What is the best sequence for taking them off?

- What does the last illustration in the book show the girl doing after playing in the snow? What do you like to do after playing in the snow?

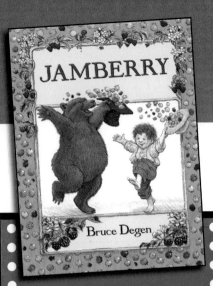

Jamberry
By Bruce Degen

Follow a loveable bear and his boy companion through their adventures in an imaginary berry-filled land.

Youngsters showcase their listening skills when they pretend to pick the array of berries in this story! Have youngsters place an imaginary hat upside down in their laps. Tell each child to listen carefully for the words *berry* and *berries* during a rereading of the book. Instruct him to pretend to pick a berry each time he hears one of the words and then drop the berry in his hat. Hats filled with berries will be picked in no time!

With this activity, students make berry-filled hats or shoes just like the ones in the story. Set out shallow containers of red, blue, and black paint. A child colors a copy of a pattern from page 65. Next, she cuts out the pattern and glues the cutout to a sheet of construction paper. Then she uses the paint to make fingerprints (berries) above and next to the cutout.

- What things in the story would not be seen in real life?

- Do you think the boy and the bear feel the same way when the canoe goes over the dam? What might each of them be thinking and feeling?

- What could be made using the different berries?

- If you were on this berry-picking adventure, which part would you like the most? Which part would you like the least?

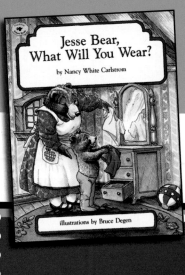

Jesse Bear, What Will You Wear?

Written by Nancy White Carlstrom and illustrated by Bruce Degen

Jesse Bear's creative (and catchy!) descriptions of his outfits provide an entertaining look at his activities one sunny day.

★ Literacy ★

With this idea, little ones categorize the sometimes unusual attire Jesse Bear wears in the story. Using a two-column chart, label one column "clothing" and the other "not clothing." During a rereading of the story, pause on each page to help youngsters identify what Jesse Bear is wearing. Ask the group to decide whether it is or is not clothing. After the correct category is determined, write the name of what Jesse is wearing in the appropriate column.

★ Literacy ★

Cut apart a copy of the cards on page 66 and display them. Read aloud a sentence starter shown, emphasizing the underlined word. Have a student identify the picture card that rhymes with that word and then flip the card over. Continue with each remaining sentence starter.

> **Sentence Starters**
> Between his <u>toes</u>, he wears a...
> On his legs that <u>run</u>, he wears the...
> He wears <u>sand</u> on his arm and...
> In his <u>hair</u>, he wears juice from a...
> He wears <u>dirt</u> all over his...
> He wears water to <u>float</u> his...

★ Story Discussion ★

- Based on the clothes Jesse Bear is wearing, what season might it be? What other details in the story tell the season?

- What does Jesse Bear eat for lunch? What does he drink? How can you tell what Jesse is drinking?

- When bedtime comes, what game does Jesse Bear play? What do you like to do before going to bed?

Kitten's First Full Moon

By Kevin Henkes

When Kitten sees a full moon for the first time, she's sure it's a big bowl of milk. Kitten's attempts to reach the moon are unsuccessful, and she ends up tired, wet, and sad. Fortunately, there is a surprise waiting for her at home. Lucky Kitten!

★ Literacy ★

Youngsters summarize this adorable story and add their summary to a marvelous moon display! Place a length of black bulletin board paper on a tabletop and use a white crayon to draw the outline of an oversize moon on the paper. Invite students to the table and encourage them to fingerpaint the moon white. When the paint is dry, display the paper. Then help students summarize the story as you write their words on chart paper. Display the chart paper next to the moon.

★ Math ★

Little ones develop patterning skills with kitten's emotions from the story. Cut out several copies of the kitten head patterns on page 67 and place them at a center. Remind youngsters that the kitten has many happy and sad moments in the story. Then encourage them to make simple patterns with the cutouts and read the patterns aloud. Poor Kitten, lucky Kitten, poor Kitten, lucky Kitten!

★ Story Discussion ★

- Why does the author use the words "poor Kitten" and "lucky Kitten"?

- What is something you've tried several times before succeeding?

- What might Kitten think the sun, stars, or clouds are?

- Is the moon always a full moon? What other shapes might it be?

Knuffle Bunny:
A Cautionary Tale
By Mo Willems

Trixie and her daddy have a relaxing outing to the laundromat until Trixie realizes that her precious Knuffle Bunny toy is missing. When her parents realize what is amiss, they rush to the laundromat and find Trixie's toy bunny.

★ Literacy ★

Encourage youngsters to revisit the story through dramatic play! Transform a box into a washing machine and place it in a center. Provide a basket of clothing, a doll (Trixie), a stuffed bunny, and a copy of the book. You may also want to provide play money for the washing machine and a clean, empty detergent bottle. Encourage students to visit the center and act out the story's plot.

★ Social ★ Studies

Little ones will enjoy making a simple map of Trixie's walk with her dad to the laundromat. Color and cut out a copy of the cards on page 68. Draw a path with a few outdoor details on a large sheet of paper. Invite youngsters to help arrange the cards in the appropriate sequence along the path. Then encourage students to take turns explaining the route Trixie and her dad take to the laundromat and back home again.

★ Story ★ Discussion

● How are this book's illustrations different from other books you have seen?

● How do you think Trixie feels as she walks with her dad to the laundromat? How do you think she feels on the way home?

● Do you have (or have you ever had) something special you like to carry with you? Did you ever leave it somewhere like Trixie? What happened?

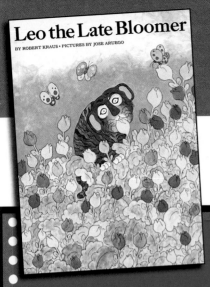

Leo the Late Bloomer
Written by Robert Kraus and illustrated by Jose Aruego

Poor Leo the tiger cannot read or write or draw. It seems that he cannot do anything right, until one day—he blooms!

Leo accomplishes many things by the end of the story. Have students dictate their accomplishments to make this attractive display! Take a photo of each child holding a bouquet of flowers. Then prompt her to name things she can do. Write her words on a card and then display the photos and cards with the title "Our Preschool Class Has Bloomed!"

With this visual reinforcement, little ones will see that Leo needs to bloom in his own good time. Discuss with youngsters that people grow at different rates and that some do things sooner, or later, than others. Then, in a child-accessible location, place a plant, such as a mum, that is getting ready to bloom. Have students observe the plant each day and point out to youngsters that individual buds bloom at different rates.

- What types of things is Leo unable to do? What might he think and feel when he tries but can't do those things?

- Who tells Leo's father to have patience? What does having patience mean? Can you tell about a time when you did or did not have patience?

- What might Leo's father think or feel when he sees that Leo cannot do the things all the other animals can do?

- What do you think helps Leo bloom?

The Little Mouse, the Red Ripe Strawberry, and the Big Hungry Bear

Written by Don and Audrey Wood and illustrated by Don Wood

A mouse tries one thing after another to save its delicious strawberry from a big, hungry bear. In the end, the mouse is tricked into sharing its strawberry with the narrator.

★ Literacy ★

With this fun idea, little ones play the role of the big, hungry bear searching for red, ripe strawberries. Label a class supply of strawberry cutouts (patterns on page 69) with letters. Then hide each strawberry. After reading the story aloud, tell youngsters a little mouse hid red, ripe strawberries all around the classroom. Encourage each child to pretend to be the big, hungry bear sniffing its way around the room in search of a strawberry. After each student finds one, have him show it to the group and identify the letter.

★ Art ★

Little ones will be eager to make a delicious-looking strawberry just like the one in the story! To make one, a child paints a large white strawberry cutout with a mixture of red paint and sugar-free, strawberry-flavored gelatin powder. She presses leaf cutouts on the wet paint near the top of the strawberry. Then she dips the round end of a toothpick in yellow paint and dabs it on the strawberry to make seeds.

★ Story Discussion ★

- The mouse and the strawberry are seen throughout the book, but the reader never sees the bear. Does the bear really exist? If so, where might it be? If not, what else might be after the mouse's strawberry?

- During a rereading of the book, pause on various pages to let students study the mouse's expression. What might the mouse be thinking and feeling?

- How else could the mouse try to hide the strawberry?

- Why does the mouse seem happy to share its strawberry with the narrator but not with the bear?

Denise Fleming

The midday meal for one very hungry mouse includes a rainbow of delicious foods!

★ **Literacy** ★

What will Mouse eat for dinner? That's for your youngsters to decide! Introduce a story sequel titled *Dinner* and name the class as the author. Then, as you reread the story, read only the color word that precedes each food and have students substitute a dinner food for each lunch food. What meal comes next? Breakfast, of course!

★ **Math** ★

Little ones are sure to agree that each food Mouse eats is a different color. But can they agree on how many different foods Mouse eats? In advance, cut out a copy of the cards on page 70 and place them on a table. Have students guess the number of foods Mouse eats. Write their guesses on chart paper. Then reread the story. Each time Mouse eats a different type of food, select a child to attach the appropriate card to the chart paper. At the end of the story, lead youngsters in counting the cards. Finally, compare the actual number of foods eaten (*nine*) to student guesses.

★ **Story Discussion** ★

● The mouse's appearance changes throughout the story. What changes and why does this happen?

● What does it mean if you're a picky eater? Do you think the mouse is a picky eater? Are you a picky eater?

● What colors of food does the mouse eat? What food do you like to eat, and what color is it?

Mouse Paint
By Ellen Stoll Walsh

Three white mice standing on a white piece of paper are nearly invisible to a lurking cat. But when the mice discover jars of red, yellow, and blue paint, they partake in some risky color mixing!

★ Literacy ★

Youngsters identify color words as they sort these paint-covered mice! Cut out several red, yellow, blue, and white copies of the mouse patterns on page 71 and place the cutouts in a bag. Label each of four pieces of white paper with a different one of the color words and place the papers on the floor. Have a child choose a mouse and name its color. Then have him place it on the paper with that color word. Continue until all the mice are sorted. Then lead students to notice how the white mice seem to disappear when they're on white paper!

★ Art ★

Youngsters engage in color mixing of their own as they re-create the mice's artistic adventure! A child glues a red, a yellow, and a blue mouse cutout (patterns on page 71) to a sheet of white construction paper. She puts small dollops of yellow and red paint near the red mouse's feet. Then she uses a paintbrush to swirl and mix the two colors to paint an orange puddle and the lower half of the mouse. Using the appropriate paint colors, she repeats the process with the remaining mice.

★ Story Discussion ★

● Why do the mice think the three jars of paint are Mouse Paint?

● What do the mice take a bath in? What do you think the dish looks like after the mice bathe in it? What might the cat do with the dish?

● Why do the mice leave a portion of the paper white at the end of the story?

Muncha! Muncha! Muncha!

Written by Candace Fleming and illustrated by G. Brian Karas

When the sun goes down and the moon comes up, three hungry bunnies fill their tummies with vegetables from Mr. McGreely's garden. As hard as he tries to protect his veggies, the motivated munchers always outsmart him!

★ Literacy ★

Youngsters will enjoy adding musical accompaniment to the repetitive words in this story. Collect simple musical instruments for each grouping of nonsense words. For example, provide rhythm sticks for "Tippy—Tippy—Tippy, Pat!" and maracas for "Muncha! Muncha! Muncha!" Give each youngster an instrument; then have students sit in groups according to instrument type. Next, read the story aloud, prompting each group to add accompaniment when its assigned words are read. No doubt little ones will be asking for future read-alouds of this story!

★ Social ★ Studies

With this fun activity, little ones find out firsthand what it's like for those mischievous munchers to sneak into Mr. McGreely's garden! Invite a child (Mr. McGreely) to sit on a chair facing away from the group. Place a carrot under the chair. To play, Mr. McGreely closes his eyes and pretends to be asleep as you signal a child (bunny) to quietly take the carrot and hide it from view. Then Mr. McGreely opens his eyes and tries to guess who took the carrot. Choose other students to fill the roles to play several rounds.

★ Story ★ Discussion

- During what part of the day do the bunnies sneak into Mr. McGreely's garden? Why do they choose that time of the day?

- Why do you think the bunnies like Mr. McGreely's garden so much?

- Review the last illustration in the book. What might Mr. McGreely be thinking and feeling? Why is he eating a carrot with the bunnies?

- Mr. McGreely is really, really angry with the bunnies. Discuss a time when you were really, really angry.

THE NAPPING HOUSE
by AUDREY WOOD
Illustrated by DON WOOD

The Napping House

Written by Audrey Wood and illustrated by Don Wood

On a dreary day, a granny, a child, and three cuddly critters take a nap. But during all the dreaming and dozing, a tiny flea creeps up on the unsuspecting nappers. No doubt this wakeful flea will put a halt to everyone's peaceful slumber!

★ Literacy ★

With this engaging activity, little ones actively participate in the story as they chime in on the predictable text. As you read the story aloud, encourage students to chant the line "where everyone is sleeping" each time it is read. When they finish chanting the line, have youngsters fold their hands beneath their head in a sleeping pose and then make their loudest snoring sounds!

★ Math ★

The weather in this story changes from rainy to sunny, but which type of weather is represented more? Ask little ones to help find out! Provide a supply of raindrop cutouts, a few die-cut suns, and Sticky-Tac adhesive. Revisit each two-page spread and invite different volunteers to attach to each spread a raindrop or a sun to indicate the weather. Then lead youngsters in counting aloud the raindrops and suns used and comparing the amounts.

★ Story ★ Discussion

● What words in the story mean the same as the word *sleeping*?

● What happens to the bed as the story progresses? What causes this to happen?

● Would you rather take a nap on a sunny day or a stormy day? Explain.

● Do you have a pet that sleeps on your bed? Do you have a favorite stuffed animal you like to take to bed?

Olivia is a lively pig with boundless energy. She builds a sand castle skyscraper, paints a modern masterpiece, and challenges everyone else to keep up with her.

★ Literacy ★

Show youngsters the pages in the story on which Olivia sports a variety of bright red clothing. Then invite your little fashion designers to create an outfit that Olivia is sure to love. Give each child a copy of page 72. Then encourage him to draw clothes on the pig and add any desired accessories to the drawing. Have him dictate words to describe what the pig is wearing. If desired, bind the finished pages together to make a class book.

★ Art ★

Convinced she can replicate artwork she saw at a museum, Olivia tries the art technique on a wall at home. Youngsters will enjoy trying the technique too! Protect a wall and the floor with inexpensive plastic tablecloths. Hang a large sheet of paper on the protected wall and set out containers of paint and paintbrushes. A child dips a brush in paint and then gently flicks it to spatter the paper. She repeats the technique until she creates a colorful masterpiece!

★ Story Discussion ★

- What does it mean when the author says Olivia is "*very good at wearing people out?*" What might you do that wears someone out?

- How do you think Olivia was able to build such a tall sand structure? Could you build a sand structure that tall? How might you be able to do it?

- What is Olivia dreaming about on the last page of the story? What is something you dream about?

One Duck Stuck

Written by Phyllis Root and illustrated by Jane Chapman

Oh no! A duck is stuck in the muck! Watch as a host of animals that live near the marsh come to help the duck get unstuck—what luck!

★ Literacy ★

There are many rhyming words used to describe the marsh, such as *pricky, sticky; swampy, chompy;* and *soggy, loggy!* Have students use these unique pairs to practice their rhyming skills. Spread some brown play dough (marsh muck) in a tray and place other small pieces of muck nearby. Say, "Pricky, sticky" and encourage a child to come up with a real or nonsense word that rhymes with the words. Then have him add a bit of muck to the marsh. Continue in the same way with different word pairs from the story until the marsh is large and mucky. That's sticky enough to trap a ducky!

★ Art ★

What might be left behind after the duck frees itself from the marsh? Why, probably just a couple feathers! Add flour to fingerpaint to give it a thick and sticky texture. Then have each youngster fingerpaint the mixture on a sheet of paper until a desired effect is achieved. Next, have each student press a few white feathers in the center of her project. That duck isn't stuck in the muck anymore!

★ Story Discussion ★

- How many animals altogether offer to help the duck? Have each student predict the number and then help students count the number of animals on the large spread near the end of the story.

- Look at the duck's expressions throughout the book. How do you think the duck feels about being stuck?

- What would you do if you were stuck in the muck?

- Which animals would you enjoy being helped by? Which animals would you not want help from? Why?

- Is this story real or pretend? How do you know?

Planting a Rainbow

By Lois Ehlert

From bulbs, seedlings, and tiny seeds, a mother and child grow a garden of flowers and plants in every color of the rainbow. After enjoying the garden all summer long, they rest assured that they can grow a rainbow again next year.

★ Literacy ★

Youngsters need to be careful listeners with this colorful activity! Make copies of the flowers on page 73 in red, orange, yellow, green, blue, and purple. Cut out the flowers and give at least one flower to each child. Read the story aloud. When the author names the colors in the garden, have each child place her flower(s) on the carpet when the appropriate color(s) is named. By the end of the story, you'll have a beautiful flower garden right in the classroom!

★ Science ★

Have youngsters plant marigold seeds just as they do in the story! Have each child plant a few seeds in a small container according to the directions on the seed package. As they do, encourage students to compare the seeds to the illustrations of the seeds in the story. When the seeds sprout, once again have youngsters compare them to the pictures. When the plants flower, ask youngsters what color of the rainbow they planted.

★ Story Discussion ★

- When rereading the story, have students help you make a list of words that may be new to them, such as *bulbs, soil, sprout, seedlings,* and *sow.* Discuss the meanings of these words.

- Why do you think gardeners use markers for plants as they do in the story?

- Does the story have any characters? Why do you think the author and illustrator decided not to show the characters?

- Why is the book called *Planting a Rainbow*?

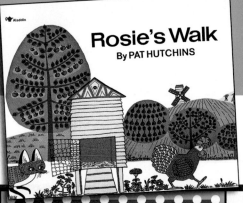

Rosie's Walk

By Pat Hutchins

Rosie the hen strolls around the farm, blissfully unaware that a fox is following her every step.

★ **Literacy** ★

Little ones will enjoy adding the fox's actions to Rosie's story. Display the opening illustration that shows Rosie starting her walk. Read the accompanying text. Then point to the fox and encourage students to describe what it is doing. Turn the page and repeat the process. Continue to the end of the story. When text does not accompany an illustration, invite little ones to describe the actions of both the hen and the fox.

★ **Math** ★

Use Rosie's actions to increase your youngsters' awareness of spatial sense. Give each child a red pom-pom or other manipulative to represent Rosie. With little ones seated on the rug, have each child move his manipulative across his lap, around his body, over his shoe, past his shoe, through his fingers, and under his legs.

★ **Story** ★
Discussion

- Ask youngsters whether they think it is smart of Rosie to take a walk by herself. Encourage them to share safety-related walking tips.

- Help little ones compare Rosie and the fox. Ask, "How are the two characters different? How are they alike?"

- Revisit the book's illustrations with the class to find the other animals, including a butterfly, frogs, mice, a bird, a goat, a grasshopper, and a whole bunch of bees! Find out whether students think any of these animals are aware that Rosie is being followed.

The Runaway Bunny

Written by Margaret Wise Brown and illustrated by Clement Hurd

When a little bunny suggests imaginative ways he might run away from his mother, she replies with equally inventive ways to find him!

★ **Literacy** ★

After reading this sweet tale of motherly love, teach your students this rhyming fingerplay that summarizes the message of the story!

Little Bunny, Little Bunny, don't run away;
Mother Bunny wants you to stay, stay, stay.
Whether you're a rock or a bird or a trout,
Your mother will find you, without a doubt!

★ **Art** ★

This is the perfect story to share around Mother's Day, but moms will appreciate this card any time of the year! To make one, have a child cut out two bunny ears and color the centers pink. Help him attach the ears to a headband. Then size the headband to fit the youngster. Take a photo of him wearing the headband and holding the book. Have him glue his photo to a card labeled "I'll always be your bunny." Then direct him to sign his name on the card.

★ **Story Discussion** ★

- Do you think the little bunny is serious about running away? What makes you think so?

- Why do you think the mother bunny is so determined to find the little bunny no matter what?

- What is a *crocus,* a *trout,* and a *trapeze?* Look at the pictures to help you figure out the meaning of these words.

- If you were trying to hide like the little bunny, what would you want to turn into?

Nancy Shaw

Sheep in a Jeep

Illustrated by Margot Apple

Sheep in a Jeep

By Nancy Shaw

What begins as fun soon turns to trouble as these unlucky sheep take a jeep for a wool-raising ride!

Literacy

No doubt your youngsters will drive a jeep better than those sheep do! Cut out a copy of the large sheep pattern on page 79. Review the words in the story that rhyme with *sheep.* Gather youngsters in a circle and place the sheep near the circle. Give each child a paper plate (steering wheel). Have students "drive" their jeeps around the circle until you say, "Brake!" The child who brakes in front of the sheep says, "Sheep, jeep, [rhyming word]." (Accept real or nonsense rhyming words.) Play continues until all the children get a chance to rhyme.

Art

These adorable sheep projects are white and fluffy, just like the sheep in the story! To make a sheep, gather a variety of white collage materials, such as tissue paper, cotton balls, pom-poms, construction paper scraps, packing peanuts, and facial tissues. Cut the materials into smaller pieces as needed. Then glue the materials on a sheep cutout (enlarge the large sheep pattern on page 79) until a desired effect is achieved.

Story Discussion

- How do you think the sheep got a jeep?

- Where do you think the sheep are going in their jeep?

- Is this story real or pretend? What makes you think so?

- What is your favorite part of the story?

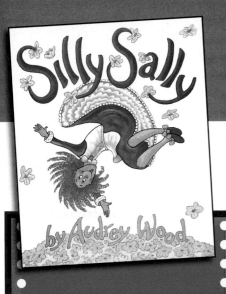

Silly Sally

By Audrey Wood

When Silly Sally goes to town, she walks backward and upside down! On the way she meets a bunch of dancing, singing, and sleeping characters that join in the fun.

Tell students that the book you're about to read is called *Silly Sally*. Encourage students to repeat the title. Then prompt youngsters to notice that both words begin with the /s/ sound. Next, say, "Sitting Sally" and prompt youngsters to notice that these two words both begin with /s/ as well. Then say, "Jumping Sally." Ask students whether both *jumping* and *Sally* begin with /s/, guiding them to notice that they do not. Repeat the process with several different made-up titles.

This group craft project also gives fine-motor skills a workout! Draw a simple, supersize picture of Sally on bulletin board paper, minus Sally's signature red, curly hair. Place the drawing at a table along with red construction paper strips, glue, and jumbo crayons or pencils. A child curls a strip by wrapping it around a crayon. Then she removes the strip and glues it to Sally's head. After each child has added several strips, display Sally so that she is upside down!

- Why do you think Sally is going to town? Why does she walk backward and upside down?

- Revisit the illustration where everyone has finally entered the town. Why do you think there is a large crowd watching them?

- Do you know anyone who can stand on his head? Have you ever tried to stand on your head?

- What other animals would you like Sally to meet?

Snow

By Uri Shulevitz

Snow-free forecasts don't hamper a boy's enthusiasm as he and his dog watch tiny snowflakes fall from the sky. One snowflake leads to another, and soon the boy and his dog are frolicking in the snow with magical friends.

★ Literacy ★

This story innovation will be a reading-center favorite! Invite each child to wear a winter hat and scarf. Then take a head-and-shoulders photo of her looking upward. Cut out the photos and have each child attach her photo to a light blue sheet of construction paper. Label the paper "'It's snowing,' ____ said." Help her write her name in the blank. Then have her dip a cotton swab in white paint and use it to make snowflake prints on the paper. Bind the pages together and read the resulting class book aloud before placing it in your reading center.

★ Math ★

Youngsters create a snowstorm and develop counting skills with this rereading of the story. Cut out several copies of the snowflake cards on page 74. Place the snowflakes on a table and prepare several pieces of tape. Begin reading the story. When the first snowflake falls, have a child attach a snowflake to the board. When two snowflakes fall, have youngsters add two more snowflakes. Continue in the same way, prompting students to add small amounts of snowflakes periodically throughout the story. At the end of the read-aloud, help students count the number of snowflakes on the board. It's snowing!

★ Story Discussion ★

- Why do you think all the characters disappear except for the boy, the dog, and the Mother Goose characters when it starts snowing heavily?

- Have you ever played in the snow? How did it make you feel?

- The illustrations in the book were made with watercolors. Have you ever painted with watercolors? Did you enjoy it?

- Does this town look anything like the town or city where you live? How is it the same? How is it different?

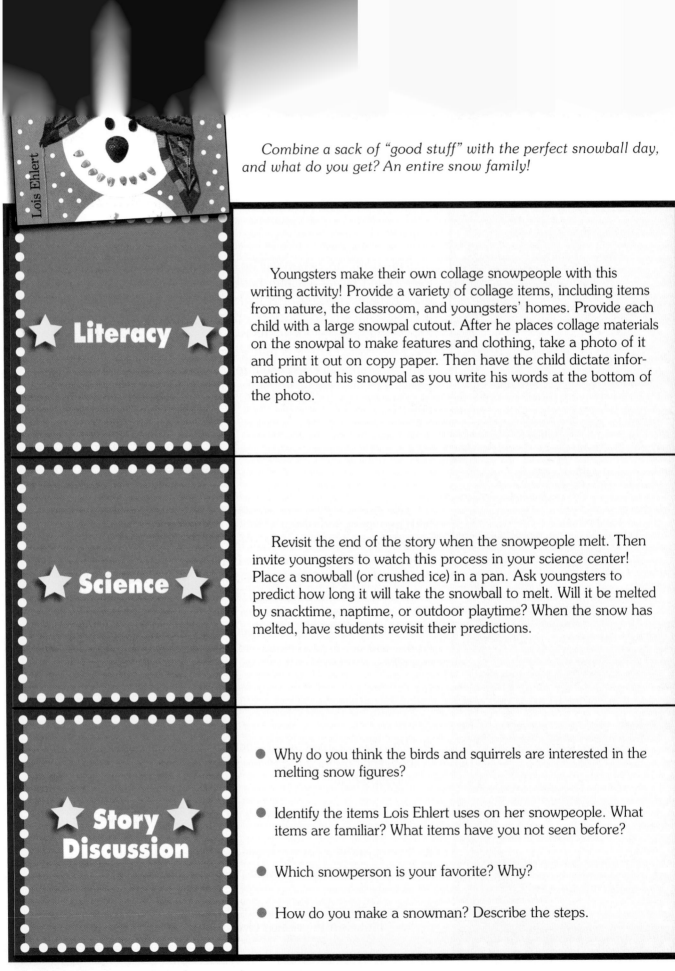

Combine a sack of "good stuff" with the perfect snowball day, and what do you get? An entire snow family!

★ Literacy ★

Youngsters make their own collage snowpeople with this writing activity! Provide a variety of collage items, including items from nature, the classroom, and youngsters' homes. Provide each child with a large snowpal cutout. After he places collage materials on the snowpal to make features and clothing, take a photo of it and print it out on copy paper. Then have the child dictate information about his snowpal as you write his words at the bottom of the photo.

★ Science ★

Revisit the end of the story when the snowpeople melt. Then invite youngsters to watch this process in your science center! Place a snowball (or crushed ice) in a pan. Ask youngsters to predict how long it will take the snowball to melt. Will it be melted by snacktime, naptime, or outdoor playtime? When the snow has melted, have students revisit their predictions.

★ Story Discussion ★

● Why do you think the birds and squirrels are interested in the melting snow figures?

● Identify the items Lois Ehlert uses on her snowpeople. What items are familiar? What items have you not seen before?

● Which snowperson is your favorite? Why?

● How do you make a snowman? Describe the steps.

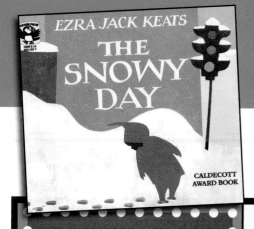

The Snowy Day

By Ezra Jack Keats

Peter wakes up one morning to discover that snow has fallen overnight. He puts on his red snowsuit and has a wonderful time exploring the snow.

Literacy

Peter certainly enjoys his time in the snow! Find out what your little ones like to do in the snow with this fun speaking activity. In advance, place youngsters' name cards in a bag. Place a white sheet or blanket (snow) on the floor and gather youngsters around it. Lead youngsters in chanting the rhyme shown. Then draw a name card. Prompt that child to sit in the snow and describe what she would like to do on a snowy day. Repeat the process for each remaining child.

Chilly, flurry, drift, and blow.
What do you do in the snow?

Gross Motor

Peter walks through the snow with his toes pointing out and then his toes pointing in. Invite little ones to do the same with this whole-group game. Place students in two lines and designate the area in front of the lines as snow. Prompt the first student in each line to walk to a specific point in the classroom with his toes pointing out. Then have each child turn around and walk to the back of his line with his toes pointing in. Continue the game until everyone has participated.

Story Discussion

- Where do you think Peter lives? What makes you think so?

- How do you think Peter feels about not joining the big boys in their snowball fight?

- Where does the snowball in Peter's pocket go?

- How could Peter have saved his snowball more successfully?

Splash!

By Ann Jonas

A little girl has some creatures that spend all their time in her pond. Other creatures, including the little girl herself, fall in and climb out. How many are in the pond now? Splash!

Literacy

Youngsters develop their own pond stories with this activity! Cut out two copies of the cards on page 75 and ready them for flannelboard use. Attach a strip of blue felt to your flannelboard so it resembles a pond. Invite a child to place critters on the pond and then ask, "How many are in my pond?" just as the little girl asks in the story. Have a classmate count the critters and name the number. Continue with several youngsters.

Math

Each spread of pages in this story offers opportunities for comparing sets. On each spread, have youngsters count the animals that are in the pond and the animals that are out of the pond. Help them compare the numbers using words such as *greater than*, *less than*, and *equal to*.

Story Discussion

- Name the animals that fall in the pond. Which animal do you think likes the water the least? Why?

- During what time of year does the story take place? What makes you think so?

- When in the story are there the most animals in the water?

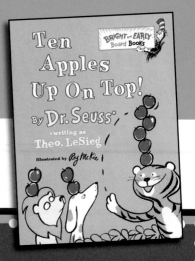

Ten Apples up on Top!

Written by Dr. Seuss and illustrated by Roy McKie

A lion, a dog, and a tiger have a balancing competition that leads to ten apples on top of each one's head. Their rollicking adventure becomes even more challenging when some bears and birds try to make the apples drop.

★ Literacy ★

Your youngsters will have apples on their own heads with this rhyming activity! Have each child color and cut out a copy of an apple (patterns on page 76). Then name pairs of words, prompting students to hold their apples above their heads whenever they hear rhyming words.

★ Math ★

Youngsters make a set of ten with a project that has them looking as if they're balancing apples—just like the characters in the book! Take a photo of each youngster. Then help him cut out his photo and glue it to a sheet of construction paper labeled "Ten Apples up on Top." Prompt him to press his thumb on a red ink pad and make a row of ten thumbprint apples above his head. Add stems and leaves to the apples. If desired, bind the projects together and place the resulting class book in your reading center.

★ Story Discussion ★

- Why do you think the dog, tiger, and lion continue to add more apples to their heads?

- What should the animals do with all the apples when they are finished balancing them on their heads?

- Do you think the animals are friends? Why or why not?

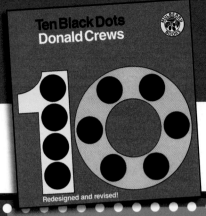

Ten Black Dots
By Donald Crews

What can you make with black dots? The spots on a snake, wheels on a train, portholes, buttons, and many other things!

Literacy

With this story, youngsters make a set of ten black dots just like the ones in the story! Provide ten black felt dots. Begin reading the book aloud, pausing before reading the rhyming word on the first page spread. Prompt youngsters to supply the word. Then have a child place a black dot on the flannelboard. Continue in the same way for each number. After you reach the pages that focus on the number 10, have students count the dots on the flannelboard. Why, there are ten!

Math

Invite little ones to make a colorful version of the book's cover as they practice counting to ten. Give each child a sheet of white construction paper with a number 10 outline. Using the book cover as a model, have students use bingo daubers to add colored dots within the number outline. Encourage students to count as they go to make sure they have exactly ten dots.

Story Discussion

● Why do you think the author decided to make all the dots black?

● What else can you make with black dots?

● Which illustration do you like best? Why?

The Very Hungry Caterpillar

By Eric Carle

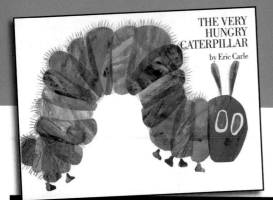

Throughout the week, this voracious caterpillar consumes a great quantity of food. Suddenly the caterpillar is no longer little, and he's ready for the next stage in his life!

★ **Literacy** ★

This story innovation is sure to delight your little ones! Write on chart paper "The very hungry preschoolers ate some food. They ate…" Then prompt each child to name a food as you write it on the chart paper. Next, have each child draw and cut out a picture of his food. Help him punch a hole in the middle of his drawing so it resembles the foods in the story. Then display the foods around the chart paper.

★ **Art** ★

This artwork is covered with very hungry caterpillars! Encourage each youngster to tear leaf shapes from green paper. Help her punch a hole in each leaf and then glue the leaf to a colorful sheet of paper. Next, prompt her to glue small pieces of green pipe cleaner (caterpillar bodies) to the leaves. Then have her attach small red pom-poms (heads) to the bodies.

★ **Story Discussion** ★

- What does it mean when someone has a big appetite? Do you think the caterpillar has a big appetite? Do you have a big appetite?

- Look at the egg on the first page of the story. Where did the egg come from? What do you think will happen to the butterfly at the end of the story?

- Have you ever had a stomachache? What made you feel better?

Wemberly Worried
By Kevin Henkes

Wemberly worries about everything, from her stuffed bunny toy to the disturbing crack in the living room wall. And when it's time for school to begin, Wemberly has a whole new set of worries!

★ Literacy ★

Hold up the book and read the title aloud, running your finger beneath the words. Prompt students to repeat the title and notice that each word begins with the letter *W*. Give each child a *W* card (patterns on page 77). Encourage her to decorate her card with stripes, just like the stripes on Wemberly's dress. Then have her transform the card into a stick puppet. Reread the story, pausing each time you say the word *worried* and prompting students to raise their puppets. That is a lot of worry!

★ Literacy ★

Wemberly has worries, and your little ones may have worries as well. Have students sit in a circle. Then give a child a stuffed bunny toy (or other stuffed toy). Encourage the child to share any worries she may have. Acknowledge her worries. Then have her pass the toy to the next youngster.

★ Story Discussion ★

- Review the illustrations of Wemberly's grandmother. Do you think her grandmother worries a lot? Do you think she is a fun grandmother? What makes you think so?

- Why do you think Mrs. Peachum wants Wemberly and Jewel to meet?

- Do you think Wemberly is having fun when she is worried? Why or why not? Is she having fun at the end of the story? Why or why not?

- Review the things that Wemberly worries about. Is there ever a real reason for her to worry about these things?

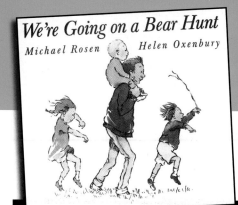

We're Going on a Bear Hunt
================================

We're Going on a Bear Hunt

Written by Michael Rosen and illustrated by Helen Oxenbury

A father and his children walk through swishy grass, a splashy river, and other noisy surroundings when they go on a bear hunt. Youngsters will particularly enjoy the humorous ending to this traditional chant.

★ **Literacy** ★

With this engaging idea, youngsters sequence the different settings encountered by the father and his children. Cut apart the cards on a copy of page 78. After a read-aloud of the story, have youngsters help you place the cards in a pocket chart in story order. Then point to each card and lead little ones in reciting the words while pretending to walk through the pictured terrain. When you reach the final card, repeat the process in reverse and with great urgency to avoid being caught by the bear!

★ **Math** ★

This classic chant uses a variety of positional words. Invite youngsters to practice similar positional words with their own classroom bear hunt! Set up a center with a simple obstacle course. For example, youngsters could go *over* a rug, *under* a table, and *through* a plastic hoop. Then place a teddy bear at the end of the course. Encourage each child to go through the obstacle course, naming the positional words as he travels. When he reaches the bear, he picks it up and takes it back through the course.

★ **Story Discussion** ★

● Why do you think the family wants to go on a bear hunt? Why do they change their minds once they find a real bear?

● Examine the illustration of the bear on the inside back cover of the book. What do you think the bear might be thinking and feeling?

● Which settings from the story would you most enjoy traveling through and which would you least enjoy? Why?

Where Is the Green Sheep?

Written by Mem Fox and illustrated by Judy Horacek

Blue sheep, red sheep, bath sheep, bed sheep! There are many different sheep, but where is the green sheep? He is discovered sleeping at the very end of the story.

★ Literacy ★

There are many unique sheep in the story. Your little ones are sure to enjoy creating more! Make a copy of the large sheep pattern on page 79. Prompt a child to share a new sheep name, using areas of your classroom and school for inspiration. For example, she might create chair sheep, puzzle sheep, or blocks sheep. Have her place the sheep in the appropriate location. Then take a photo of the sheep. Print out the photos on copy paper and label each page with the sheep's name. Then bind the pages together. Youngsters are sure to enjoy this story extension!

★ Literacy ★

Youngsters review letter names while they search for the green sheep! Cut out several copies of the small sheep patterns on page 79. Color one sheep green and then place the sheep in your pocket chart. Cover each sheep with a different letter card. Lead youngsters in saying, "Where is the green sheep?" Then have a child name one of the letters and remove the card. If the card reveals the green sheep, say, "There it is!" If it does not, repeat the question again and choose another volunteer.

★ Story Discussion ★

- Can sheep really do all the things they can in this story? What can sheep do? Is this story real or pretend?

- Have you ever touched a sheep? How did it feel? (Or how do you imagine it would feel?)

- Why do you think Mem Fox writes about sheep in her story? What animal would you choose to write about?

WHERE THE WILD THINGS ARE

STORY AND PICTURES BY MAURICE SENDAK

Where the Wild Things Are

By Maurice Sendak

When Max gets into trouble, his mother calls him a Wild Thing and sends him to his room without supper. That night, he becomes king of the Wild Things and leads them in a wild rumpus! But soon he is lonely and goes back to the place he is loved best of all.

★ Literacy ★

Youngsters practice listening skills when they add musical accompaniment to the story! Give each child a simple rhythm instrument, such as rhythm sticks or a tambourine. Begin to read the story. When you come to the line describing how the Wild Things roar their roars, gnash their teeth, roll their eyes, and show their claws, encourage students to play their instruments. Prompt them to play during the wild rumpus and again when the previously mentioned line is repeated.

★ Gross Motor ★

With this idea, each youngster gets a turn being a Wild Thing! Have a child name a movement, such as jumping up and down or marching. Then place a paper crown on the child's head and encourage her to say, "Let the wild rumpus start!" Encourage students to repeat the movement several times. Then prompt the child to say, "Go to bed!" and encourage youngsters to gently fall to the floor and pretend to sleep. Repeat the activity several times, choosing a new volunteer for each round.

★ Story Discussion ★

● Revisit the pages at the beginning of the story. What type of mischief is Max making? Why does it bother his mother? Is he punished enough?

● Why isn't Max afraid of the Wild Things?

● Do you think Max will make mischief again? Why or why not?

● This book won an award called the Caldecott Medal. The Caldecott Medal is given to good picture books with excellent pictures. Do you think this book deserves the medal? What book would you give a medal to?

Wiggle

Written by Doreen Cronin and illustrated by Scott Menchin

An exuberant little pup invites readers to wiggle with various objects and creatures from early in the morning until late at night, when it runs out of wiggles and falls asleep beneath the moon.

★ Literacy ★

Invite students to wiggle with different creatures with this rhyming activity! Cut out a copy of the cards on page 80 and place them faceup on your floor. Gather youngsters around the cards. Have a child choose a card and name the picture. Then prompt another child to find the rhyming picture. Have the youngsters stand. Then, inserting the appropriate picture names, ask, "Can you wiggle with a [dog]? Can you wiggle with a [frog]?" Prompt the students to hold their cards and wiggle. Then have them place the cards aside. Repeat the activity for each card pair.

★ Art ★

This wiggly art project is sure to be a hit with your little ones! Provide shallow pans of colorful paint and place a bath pouf next to each pan. Have each youngster choose a pouf. Then chant, "Wiggle, wiggle, wiggle," as the child wiggles the pouf over a sheet of paper. Continue with other colors of paint until a desired effect is achieved.

★ Story ★ Discussion

- Why do you think the dog in this story is so wiggly?

- Revisit the illustrations. What do you notice about certain items such as the alarm clock, the pancakes, and the bird's nest?

- Who or what would you like to wiggle with?

- Do you ever get wiggly? What makes you wiggly?

TEC61315

TEC61315

TEC61315

TEC61315

TEC61315

TEC61315

TEC61315

TEC61315

Cap Pattern •
Use with the literacy activity on page 11.

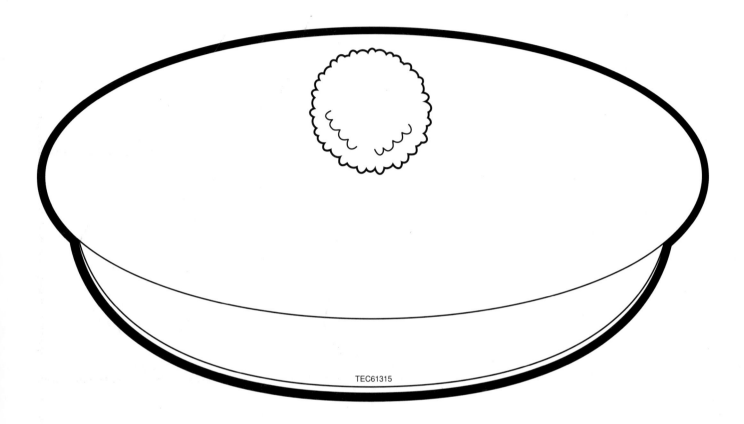

TEC61315

Monkey and Cap Cards • • • • • • • • • • • • • • • • •
Use with the math activity on page 11.

TEC61315 | TEC61315 | TEC61315 | TEC61315

TEC61315 | TEC61315 | TEC61315 | TEC61315

Read-Aloud Roundup • ©The Mailbox® Books • TEC61315

TEC61315

TEC61315

TEC61315

TEC61315

TEC61315

TEC61315

TEC61315

TEC61315

TEC61315

TEC61315

TEC61315

TEC61315

Picture Cards

Use with the first literacy activity on page 13.

TEC61315

TEC61315

TEC61315

TEC61315

TEC61315

TEC61315

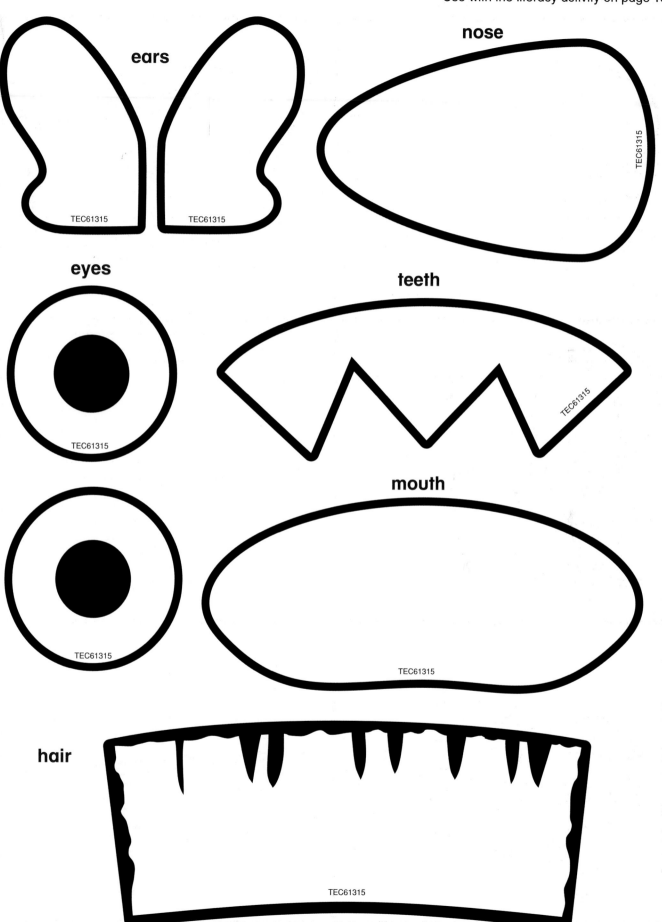

ears

nose

TEC61315

TEC61315

TEC61315

eyes

teeth

TEC61315

TEC61315

mouth

TEC61315

TEC61315

hair

TEC61315

Note to the teacher: Use with the literacy activity on page 19.

TEC61315

TEC61315

TEC61315

Animal Patterns

Use with the second literacy activity on page 21.

TEC61315

TEC61315

TEC61315

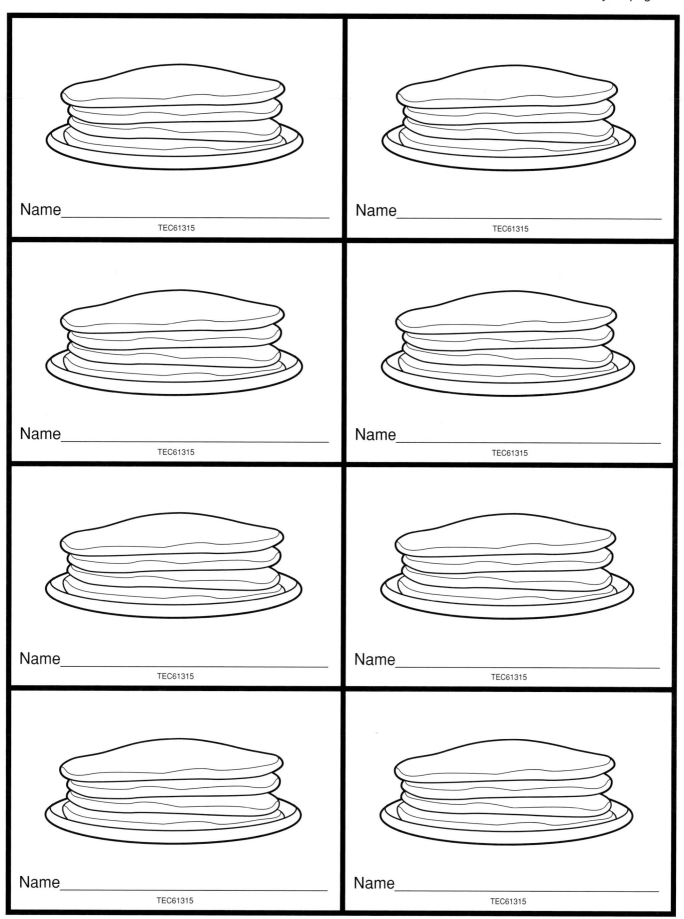

Animal Cards ● ● ● ● ● ● ● ● ● ● ● ● ● ● ● ● ● ● ●

Use with the science activity on page 23.

TEC61315

TEC61315

TEC61315

TEC61315

TEC61315

TEC61315

Read-Aloud Roundup • ©The Mailbox® Books • TEC61315

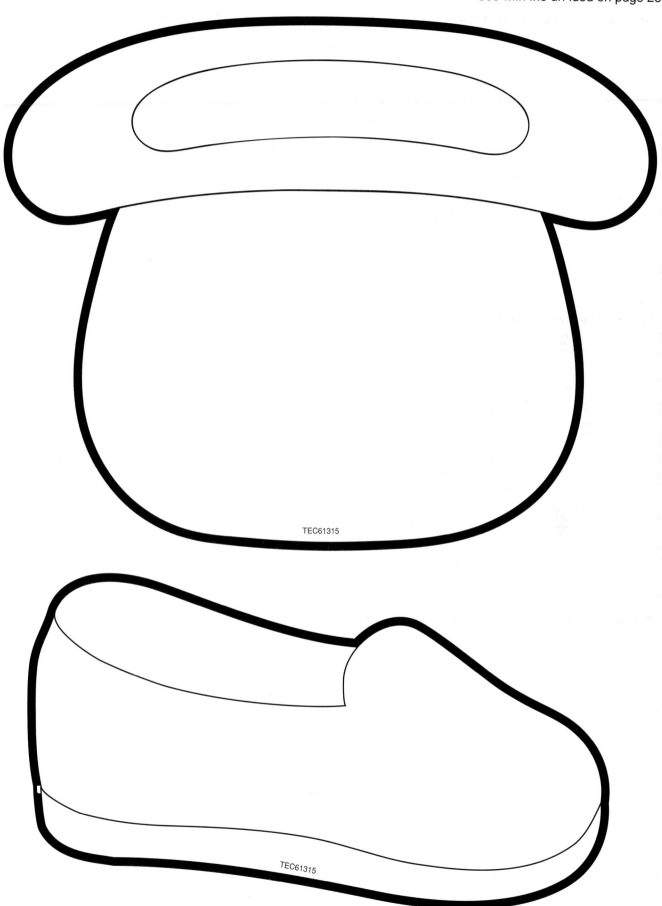

TEC61315

TEC61315

Picture Cards •

Use with the second literacy activity on page 27.

TEC61315

TEC61315

TEC61315

TEC61315

TEC61315

TEC61315

TEC61315

TEC61315

Picture Cards

Use with the social studies activity on page 29.

TEC61315

TEC61315

342

School

TEC61315

TEC61315

TEC61315

TEC61315

TEC61315

TEC61315

Picture Cards •

Use with the math activity on page 32.

TEC61315

TEC61315

TEC61315

TEC61315

TEC61315

TEC61315

TEC61315

TEC61315

TEC61315

TEC61315

TEC61315

TEC61315

TEC61315

Snowflake Cards •

Use with the math activity on page 43.

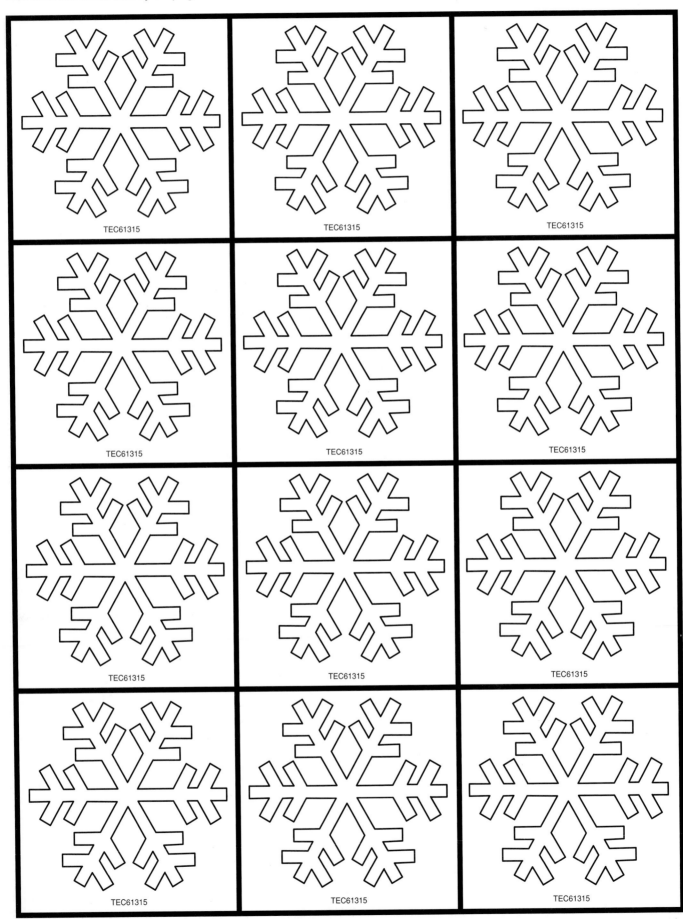

TEC61315   TEC61315   TEC61315

TEC61315   TEC61315   TEC61315

TEC61315   TEC61315   TEC61315

TEC61315   TEC61315   TEC61315

TEC61315

TEC61315

TEC61315

TEC61315

TEC61315

TEC61315

Use with the literacy activity on page 47.

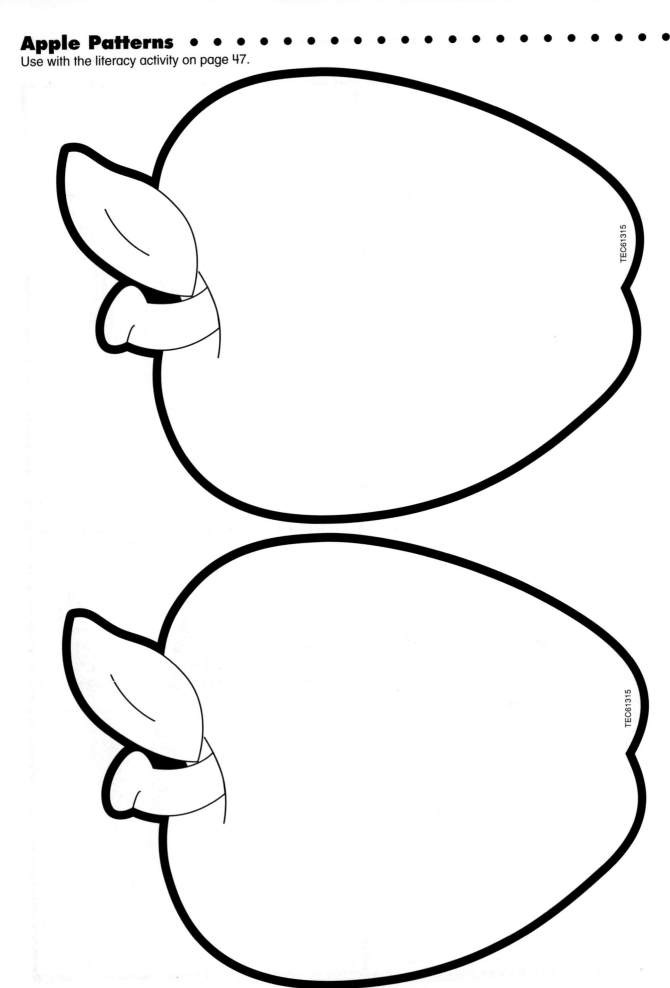

TEC61315

TEC61315

Read-Aloud Roundup • ©The Mailbox® Books • TEC61315

TEC61315

TEC61315

TEC61315

TEC61315

Swishy swashy!

TEC61315

Splash splosh!

TEC61315

Squelch squerch!

TEC61315

Stumble trip!

TEC61315

Hoooo woooo!

TEC61315

Tiptoe! Tiptoe!

TEC61315

Large Sheep Pattern

Use with the literacy and art ideas on page 41 and the first literacy idea on page 52.

TEC61315

Small Sheep Patterns

Use with the second literacy idea on page 52.

TEC61315

TEC61315

Picture Cards •

Use with the literacy idea on page 54.

TEC61315

TEC61315

TEC61315

TEC61315

TEC61315

TEC61315

TEC61315

TEC61315

TEC61315

TEC61315

TEC61315

TEC61315

Read-Aloud Roundup • ©The Mailbox® Books • TEC61315